Chinas, Mario.

MARKET EFFICIENCY: DAY OF THE WEEK EFFECT

Introduction to Weak Form Efficiency for Business Students

Includes bibliographical references.

ISBN: 978-9925-7383-2-8

Webpage: https://www.mccebooks.com

TABLE OF CONTENTS

PREFACE 3

GLOSSARY 4

INTRODUCTION 5

THEORY 6

    FUNDAMENTAL & TECHNICAL ANALYSIS..11

    RANDOM WALK...12

    DEFINITIONS OF MARKET EFFICIENCY..13

    WEAK FORM EFFICIENCY...15

DAY-OF-THE-WEEK EFFECTS...17

WEAK FORM MARKET EFFICIENCY TESTS.............................23

    1. REGRESSION ANALYSIS - GENERAL INDEX AGAINST TIME.............24

    2. REGRESSION ANALYSIS - DAY RELATIONSHIPS 25

    3. OTHER PARAMETRIC STATISTICAL TOOLS 25

    4. NON-PARAMETRIC TESTS (RUNS TESTS) 27

END NOTE 29

REFERENCES & BIBLIOGRAPHY 31

OTHER BOOKS BY THE AUTHOR...33

PREFACE

Welcome to the 1st edition of Market Efficiency: Day of the Week effect. This book introduces Weak Form Efficiency via a specific anomaly, the Day of the Week effect. We cover the fundamental theory of the topic in question in a clear and concise manner.

This book covers the basic fundamentals of capital markets, the setting of stock prices in stock exchanges, random walk theory, and moves on to the concept of market efficiency and the Efficient Market Hypothesis. We then look at the Day of the Week effect, a specific anomaly in weak form efficiency. Lastly we look at market efficiency tests and make further discussion on weak form efficiency tests.

Our series of Books for Business Students are concise and targeted to maximizing your 'value for time', i.e. to give you the maximum essential learning on the subject matter in the shortest time.

As you will notice, our Books are written in a style and format that emulates essay writing. The aim is to familiarise you, the reader, with the format and style expected in essay writing, providing a bridge between the study material and the output you will be expected to deliver in your essay projects and essay based exams. Moreover they provide a wealth of references / bibliography, saving you valuable time that you can utilise to further enhance your work.

GLOSSARY

Abnormal returns - a term used to describe returns that are higher/lower than the expected returns.

Blue chip - a share that is costly and of good quality.

Efficient Market Hypothesis (EMH) - is defined as the Hypothesis that stocks already reflect all available information.

IPO - Initial public offering; the first public offer of shares by a company.

Positivistic paradigm - describes a research based on quantitative data.

Random walk hypothesis - is defined as the Hypothesis that stock prices should follow a random walk, i.e. they should be random and unpredictable.

Return, (daily return) - The gain/loss in the Index in comparison to the previous day.

Shares - ownership rights in companies, bought and sold in the form of printed statements. For the purposes of this dissertation companies will equate with public limited companies.

Weak Form Market Efficiency - is defined as the Hypothesis that stock prices already reflect all information that can be derived by examining market trading data such as the history of past prices and trading volume, implying that trend analysis is fruitless.

INTRODUCTION

In an efficient stock market all relevant information regarding a given stock should be reflected in its market price. Market Efficiency has to do with the speed with which new information is incorporated into the stock price. A market can be regarded as efficient, with regard to a particular set of information, if investors using that information will receive the return expected for the risk involved.

The Efficient Market Hypothesis is defined as 'the notion that stocks already reflect all available information', and is separated into three versions: weak, semi-strong, and strong, depending on the definition of "all available information" (Bodie et al, 1996, p. 340-341).

In this book, we will review the relevant theories behind Market Efficiency and the Efficient Market Hypothesis and examine in more detail a specific market efficiency anomaly; the Day-of-the-week effect. We will then look at some examples of Weak Form Market Efficiency Tests.

We will begin with a general overview of the functioning of the stock market, the determination of stock prices and stock market efficiency.

THEORY

The capital market is the place where stocks are traded. It consists of two parts: the primary market where new stocks are bought and sold, and the secondary market where existing stocks are traded (Worthington & Britton, 1994, p. 186). The main institution in the capital market is the Stock Exchange; Stock Exchanges (or stock markets) are defined as 'secondary markets where already-issued securities [i.e. stocks] are bought and sold by members [a member is the holder of an 'exchange position' which enables the holder to trade for the holder's own accounts and charge clients for the execution of trades for their accounts], (Boddie et al, 1996, p. G12).

The aim of the stock market is to provide long term finance to companies; 'The fact that from the point of view of the individual saver it is only be intended to be a short- term loan does not limit the possible ways of using it as much as one might think. For even though the individual savings are only saved for a temporary period, collectively they may in large part be looked upon as long-term savings of the economic system' (Machlup, 1940, p.255). The probability that new savings will be sufficient to cover withdrawals of old savings is what makes it possible to invest these short-term funds into long-term projects. 'The system whereby this investment is made through the stock exchange has special advantages, for in this case the transformation of what are short-term credits from the private viewpoint into long-term savings from the social viewpoint can take place to the fullest extent...' (Machlup, 1940, p.255).

The securities markets are characterised by a number of properties that render them especially suitable to serve as capital resource allocators. First, they offer guidance to business management, by providing information on the current cost of capital, which is important in determining the level of investment that is appropriate for the firm to undertake.

Second, the securities markets offer the advantage of accessibility to vast numbers of investors, many of who possess only small amounts of money and yet who in their aggregate have command over vast quantities of wealth.

Third, 'the markets offer a simple mechanism for the transfer of funds that imposes only a minimum of administrative effort upon the lender' (Baumol, 1965, p. 3). Fourth, stock markets offer the investor an easily understood evaluation of the financial condition and the future prospects of the borrowing firm as indicated by the market price of its securities and by movements in the magnitude of that price.

Finally, as we have seen, 'the market performs an act of magic, for it permits long-term investments to be financed by funds provided available by individuals, many of whom wish to make them available for only a very limited period, or who wish to be able to withdraw them at will' (Baumol,1965, p. 3).

The organisation and size of stock markets differ from one country to another, but 'all are dealing with instruments representing claims of ownership, sometimes with qualification, to enterprises of industrial, financial, and service character' (Granger & Morgenstern, 1970, p.1). The results of the activities of the stock market are chiefly described by the recorded price movements; 'the prices assigned to stocks by the free market are critical to the effectiveness of the market as a resource allocator' (Baumol, 1965, p. 7).

Stock prices depend on investor expectations of the performance of the company, which affect the demand and supply of the stock and thus the equilibrium price at which it is traded. Based on their expectations, investors speculate on the future performance of the stock and act accordingly; speculation is an emotionally laden word and thus to a large extend depends on the eye of the beholder (Granger, 1970, p. 34).

As Granger (1970) points out, there is a relationship between stock market activity and gambling; both deal with speculation. Granger states that 'all economic activity is speculative when it is not completely deterministic and there is no such thing. There are only degrees of uncertainty and there is no sharp, scientifically established line where acceptable and unacceptable risk-taking is separated, either for the individual or for society. All economic activity is directed into the future, from the next hour to the next decade; all depends on expectations and all are uncertain in various manners' (p. 35).

It follows that stock prices should incorporate market expectations concerning a variety of macro and micro economic factors, such as interest rates, dividends, discount rates, growth of the economy & the relevant industry, company performance, and so on, which affect the demand and supply of a stock (Rutterford, 1994).

'It is generally recognised that an efficient stock market should value a company's stock in some way on the basis of the capitalised value of the company's earnings potential' (Baumol, 1965, p. vii). Therefore, in an efficient stock market all relevant information regarding a given stock is reflected in its market price, that is, the price of a stock will reflect the markets best estimates of their expected return and risk, taking into account all that is known about them. There will thus be no undervalued stocks offering higher than deserved expected return, given their risk (i.e.

fair return for risk). Note that 'a weaker and economically more sensible version of the efficiency hypothesis says that prices reflect information to the point where the marginal benefits of acting on information (the profits to be made) do not exceed the marginal costs' (Fama, 1991, p. 1575).

Grossman & Stiglitz (1980) challenged this view of market equilibrium, by asserting that if prices are such that all arbitrage profits are eliminated, then there is no benefit for those who arbitrage; i.e. there is no return from the costly information. Grossman & Stiglitz propose a model in which there is an equilibrium degree of disequilibrium: 'prices reflect the information of informed individuals (arbitrageurs) but only partially, so that those who expend resources to obtain information do receive compensation. How informative the price system is depends on the number of individuals who are informed' (p. 393).

This model conveys information from the informed to the uninformed for a cost; the cost is the 'extra' return received by the informed. Information is conveyed through the price system; when informed individuals observe information that the return to a security is going to be high, they bid the price up, and when they observe information that the return is going to be low, they bid the price down.

If a market is inefficient, then excess returns can be made by identifying the undervalued stocks. The market is considered inefficient if some investors know something about a stock that the market does not (e.g. insider dealings), or if the market has not yet incorporated the information into the share price. It should be noted that most investment advisers act as if markets are inefficient and that therefore excess profits can be made, through security analysis (Rutterford, 1988, p. 253).

FUNDAMENTAL & TECHNICAL ANALYSIS

There are two kinds of security analysis; fundamental and technical. Fundamental analysis seeks to forecast each stocks return by studying the prospects for each company's business, through factors such as the state of the economy, demand for a company's goods, the company's balance sheet and income statement, etc. Technical analysis on the other hand attempts to forecast the return by searching for patterns in past stock prices. The analysts in this group use charts and graphs of past price data, and are therefore called chartists. In practice most institutional investors use a mix of charts and fundamental analysis.

In an efficient market, as new items of information about a stock comes in, the share price absorbs this information and moves to a new equilibrium. The market is seen as an efficient information processor, so that any new information will cause prices to adjust quickly to that new information (Tarascio, 1984). Thus, ceteris paribus, until new information is released, the share price can be considered to be at equilibrium.

Any new information, good or bad, will be independent of the previous piece of information, or otherwise it would not be new. Therefore the new price change will be independent from previous price changes.

RANDOM WALK

Thus, it can be concluded that share prices follow a random walk; that is, price changes are independent of each other, and consequently there are no trends in price changes. For the more mathematically inclined, $P_{t+1} - P_t$ is independent of $P_t - P_{t-1}$, where 'P is the price of the share at time t' (Rutterford, 1988, p. 284). 'There are a number of ways in which this model may be stated but the most natural form is:

$$P_t = P_{t-1} + E_t$$

Where P_t is price at time t, P_{t-1} is price at time t-1, and E_t is the residual at time t. It should be noted that the residual series has zero mean and is uncorrected with all previous terms in the residual series' (Granger & Morgenstern, 1970, p. 71).

If the model holds, then it follows that 'the best predictor of tomorrow's price is today's price or, putting it equivalently another

way: price changes cannot be predicted from previous prices'
(Granger & Morgenstern, 1970, p. 71).

'The idea that security prices in a organised market might follow a
random walk was first put forward by Bachelier in 1900 for
commodities traded on the French commodities market'
(Rutterford, 1994, p.284).

One point that should be noted is that in the real world, share
prices exhibit an upward trend, and therefore 'the equilibrium price
is expected to move upwards in the future, assuming no new
information is released to affect the price' (Rutterford, 1988, p.
255).

DEFINITIONS OF MARKET EFFICIENCY

As stated before, in an efficient stock market all relevant
information regarding a given stock is reflected in its market price.

But what is relevant information? There are three alternative
definitions of market efficiency, depending on what you consider
to be relevant information (Fama, 1970; Fama, 1991):

Weak Form Market Efficiency - exists if stock prices
approximate a random walk, and knowledge of past price
changes is no predictor of future price changes. If the market

is Weak Form efficient then no amount of charts or analysis based solely on past prices can help to obtain abnormal profit.

Semi-strong Form Market Efficiency - the market is Semi-strong efficient if all publicly available information of the relevant stock is reflected in the stock price. If a market is Semi-strong Form efficient then one cannot make abnormal profits by looking at any publicly available information, such as firm announcements and past prices.

Strong Form Market Efficiency - the market is Strong-form efficient if all information, including non-public (insider) information of the relevant stock, is reflected in the stock price. Thus, any information, including private information, is worthless, and it is impossible for an individual to achieve abnormal profits.

In all three cases Market Efficiency has to do with the speed with which new information is incorporated into the stock price. A market can be regarded as efficient, with regard to a particular set of information, if investors using that information will receive the return expected for the risk involved.

In order to ascertain if a stock market is efficient, you must test it for each level of efficiency. There are distinct methods for testing each level of efficiency, stated in the table below, however we will later look further into Weak Form efficiency tests, since this is the most researched area and of course the easiest to research.

Table Efficiency Tests:
1. Weak Form Market Efficiency:
- *Random Walk Tests*
- *Runs Tests*
- *Filter Rules Tests*

2. Semi-Strong Form Market Efficiency:
- *Stock splits*
- *Brokerage house recommendations*

3. Strong Form Market Efficiency:
- *Performance of insider investors*
- *Performance of mutual funds*

WEAK FORM EFFICIENCY

In order to determine if a market is Weak Form efficient, tests are carried out to ascertain if patterns exist in stock price movements.

The random walk hypothesis stipulates that stock prices should follow a random walk, 'that is, that price changes should be random and unpredictable' (Bodie et al, 1996, p. 339). The Random Walk hypothesis is tested by looking for association between stock price changes on consecutive days. The runs test serves the same purpose, through non-parametric testing. The Filter Rule test on the other hand, tests for relationships in individual stock price movements, irrespective of the time at which they occur. It should be noted that Random Walk and Runs Tests can be performed for individual stocks also, and that there are numerous tests that fall under these two categories.

Proof of the random walk theory can take various forms. As with all tested theories involving future expected prices or returns, past actual prices or returns are used for the tests. That is, sets of past share prices are tested for dependence in order to test the random walk theory.

DAY-OF-THE-WEEK EFFECTS

The two decades following the development of the capital asset pricing model (Sharp, 1964; Litner, 1965) saw an explosion in work investigating both asset pricing models and market efficiency (Fama, 1970; Ross, 1976). This was followed by a decade characterised by an almost relentless search for anomalies in stock returns (Elsharkawyand & Garrod, 1996; Connolly, 1991). The major anomalies in stock returns that have been documented are: the size/January effect, the monthly effect, and the weekend effect (Elsharkawyand & Garrod, 1996; Connolly, 1991).

Weekend effect - Defined as: 'the tendency for Monday stock returns to be negative' (Connolly, 1991, p. 51). Although other day-of-the-week effects have been identified, this is by far the most widespread anomaly in this category. Thus it is not surprising that most research focuses around this anomaly.

Ever since Cross (1973) observed that stock returns are higher than average on the last trading day of the week and lower than average on the first, many researchers have documented and attempted to explain the reason(s) behind this pattern. The word anomaly is avoided here because certain theories claim that the pattern is an efficient one and propose explanations for the phenomenon; we will examine these theories later on.

The term "day-of-the-week effect" is used to refer to the anomaly of a certain day having higher/lower than average returns, or 'that the distribution of common stock returns varies by day of the week' (Keim & Stambaugh, 1984, p. 819). Thus the weekend effect is a type of day-of-the-week effect anomaly. For clarity we will use the term 'Monday effect' when referring to the tendency for Monday stock returns to be negative.

The Monday and Friday effects were first documented by Cross (1973) in the US stock markets. However, the Monday effect has a much longer history; Bessembinder & Hertzel (1993) and Lakonishok & Smidt (1989) find evidence of its existence in records that begin in 1885 and 1897 respectively.

Evidence of the Monday effect using close-to-close returns is documented in French (1980), Gibbons & Hess (1981) and Lakonishok & Levi (1982), while evidence using close-to-open, hourly, and transaction data has also been presented (Rogalski, 1984; Harris, 1986; Smirlock & Stark, 1986).

Al-Loughani & Chappell (2001) showed the Monday and Friday effect existing in the Kuwait market. Likewise, Nath & Dalvi (2004, in Rahman, 2009) investigated the stock market of India and concluded that there are specific patterns on the Monday and Friday returns.

While the Monday effect has been reported in the US and in large European stock markets, some smaller European markets have shown negative returns on Tuesdays; examples include Finland (Martikainen & Puttonen, 1996); Greece (Alexakis and Xanthakis, 1995); Spain (Santamases, 1986); Sweden (Claesson, 1987) and Ireland (Lucey, 1994). Similarly, the Tuesday effect has also been found in Asian stock markets of all sizes. This has been documented by Jaffe & Westerfield (1985) for Japan and Australia, by Lee (1990) for Japan, Korea, and Singapore, and Lai et al (2011) for the Shenzhen (Hong Kong) stock market. Furthermore, Raj & Dheeriya (1997) have identified both a Tuesday and Friday effect in Thailand. Moreover, Athanassakos & Robinson (1994) have found both a weekend/Monday and a Tuesday effect in Canada.

The Monday effect is the most widely discussed, and several researches have tried to provide explanations for it. The following explanations have been investigated and rejected as false: this effect is not the result of measurement errors in recorded prices (Gibbons & Hess, 1981; Keim & Stambaugh, 1984); it is not caused by a delay between trading and settlement dates due to cheque clearing (Gibbons & Hess, 1981); and it is not due to specialist induced bias (Keim & Stambaugh, 1984).

Other explanations seem to partially explain the weekend effect, although even this is debatable. One such explanation is the 'high Friday return hypothesis' (Keim & Stambaugh, 1984; Harris, 1986). This theory suggests that it is the Friday effect that is the anomaly, and that on Mondays stock prices return to their 'norm'. However this fails to explain why Mondays are lower than all other days of the week.

Another theory that tries to explain the Monday effect is the 'individual trader decision making process' (Miller, 1988), and an extrapolation of this is the 'investor psychology' theory (Rystrom & Benson, 1988). The first theory suggests that investors are more likely to make a sell decision over the weekend, while the second suggests the existence of a 'Blue Monday' syndrome, where investors expect prices to fall, and consequently bring about the fall themselves.

Miller's theory using the 'individual trader decision making process' suggests that there is a tendency for self-initiated sell orders to exceed self-initiated buy orders over the weekend. This theory is supported by the findings of Lakonishok & Maberly (1990), who found that in the US markets Mondays have the lowest trading volumes but the highest individual trading relative to the other days of the week.

A further explanation for both the Monday and Friday effect, is the timing of corporate announcements; Patell & Wolfson (1982) and Penman (1987) find that it is more likely for bad news to be announced over the weekend, and for good news to be announced during the week. This was first suggested by French (1980), as the 'Information Timing Hypothesis'. French suggested that firms have a tendency to release negative information over the weekends. This hypothesis is supported by Patell & Wolfson's and Penman's finding on the timing of corporate announcements. Furthermore Lakonishok & Smidt (1988) and Athanassakos & Robinson (1994) find that there is a clustering of ex-dividend days on Mondays.

Therefore, assuming the 'Information Timing Hypothesis' is true, it would be expected that good news during the week will lead prices up, with a peak on Fridays, and bad news over the weekends would bring them down again on Mondays.

Smirlock and Starks (1986) found that the Monday effect in the US has changed with time. The Monday effect for the period 1963-68 occurred during the entire trading day. However, for 1974-83 it occurs only during the first hours of trading. If the 'Information Timing Hypothesis' holds, then this could be interpreted as a decline in the markets response time to bad news released over the weekend. This is also supported by Hand (1990) whose empirical results show that the level of investor sophistication conditions the response of prices to earnings information. This decline in response time however should not exist in smaller markets with thin trading; this would explain the Tuesday effect in small European markets.

Moving on to the Tuesday effect, Ziemba & Schwartz (1992) suggest that it may be due to delays in re-entering the market at the start of the week. That is, due to thin trading on Mondays, the markets may be slow at showing the effect. Another theory, presented by Condoyianni (1987), suggests that the Tuesday effect seen in Europe and Asia is simply a reflection of the US Monday effect, which due to the difference in the time zones appears on Tuesdays. This is called the 'Time Zone' theory. However this theory fails to explain the Tuesday effect in Canada (which has the same time zone as the US), as well as the Monday effect in the UK, Israel, etc. (which are in the same time zone as the rest of Europe).

Concluding, the literature on the Day-of-the-Week effect deduces that stock returns are not homogeneously distributed over the days of the week. The most favoured explanation for this anomaly is the 'Information Timing Hypothesis'. Furthermore, it seems logical to assume that the 'investor psychology' theory may be a side effect of the 'Information Timing Hypothesis'; that is, the 'Information Timing Hypothesis' may cause the investors to expect these anomalies.

WEAK FORM MARKET EFFICIENCY TESTS

As we have seen, Weak Form Efficiency is one of the three versions of the Efficient Market Hypotheses. The Weak form Hypothesis 'asserts that stock prices already reflect all information that can be derived by examining market trading data such as the history of past prices, trading volume, or short interest', implying that 'trend analysis is fruitless' (Bodie et al, 1996, p. 341).

As stated previously, the Random Walk hypothesis is usually tested by looking at the association between stock price changes on consecutive days. The tests fall into two broad groups: parametric tests (regression analysis) and non-parametric tests (runs test). There are literally hundreds of ways with which stock price changes can be tested for, however we will briefly look at the basic tests suggested in the bibliography that relate to commonly examined weak form inefficiencies, through analysis of the all-share index.

1. REGRESSION ANALYSIS - GENERAL INDEX AGAINST TIME

The simplest way to test the random walk theory is by drawing a scatter diagram, and performing a single variable regression (explain y-variable in terms of x-variable). A scatter diagram is a graph on which you plot the points of the variable you want to explain on the vertical axis (y-variable), and the explanatory variable on the horizontal axis (x-variable).

A single variable regression aims to find the best relationship between y and x, by finding the curve (of specified type) that passes closest to the data points. By drawing a linear regression line we can find the relationship between the two variables. The equation will be of type:

$$y = a + b*x + e$$

Where 'y' will be the return on day 't', 'x' will represent time, 'a' a constant (equals the value of y when the value of x=0), 'e' the error in predicting the value of y (it is usually not displayed in most regression equations), and 'b' (also called the beta) represents the slope of the curve; the slope is the increase or decrease in height per unit of movement along the horizontal axis.

For the random walk hypothesis to hold, there should be no trend in the time-return relationship - that is, a linear regression line drawn through the points should have a slope equal, or close to, zero. Otherwise, a trend will exist, which could be used to predict future price changes (Levy, 1984).

2. REGRESSION ANALYSIS - DAY RELATIONSHIPS

Another linear regression analysis would be to plot a scatter diagram of returns on day t with returns on day t-1. If a pattern can be identified (regression line with a positive or negative slope) then this would suggest that there is a correlation between the two variables, and therefore past price change patterns can be used to predict future price movements. This method is used by chartists (Levy, 1984, pp. 670).

3. OTHER PARAMETRIC STATISTICAL TOOLS

Measures of central tendency indicate the typical (average) number for a series of data. The three main measures of central tendency are:

Mode - It is the most frequently encountered value in the sample.

Median - The sample mean is the middle observation; that is, the middle number of the data series when listed in ascending order.

Mean - The arithmetic mean is the sum of numbers included in a given sample divided by the number of observations.

Although the Mode is of little use, the other two tests of central tendency are quite useful since they will indicate if uniformity exists between the returns of each day.

In addition to knowing the typical value for a data sample, it is also useful to know the degree of variance around that value; that is, how dispersed the data is around the typical value. One such test is the Range, which is the difference from the largest to the smallest value in the data set.

Another very useful measure of dispersion is the Variance, which measures deviation throughout the sample. The Standard deviation is the square root of the Variance, and describes the dispersion throughout the sample in the same units as the data, which makes it possible for comparisons to be made between the dispersion and the data, or other tests. It is a useful tool because it will tell us which set of data is more variable; the range gives us the extreme values but does not take into account the whole sample (Bancroft & O'Sullivan, 1993).

Lastly, the correlation coefficient measures the 'goodness' of the fit for a simple regression model. That is, how well the data fits on the regression line. Its values range from -1 to 1, where:

If there is no linear relationship between the two variables then the value is zero.

If there is a perfectly inverse relationship between the variables, then the value is -1.

If there is a perfectly linear relationship between the variables, then the value is 1.

The correlation squared is called the coefficient of determination; it tells us the proportion of the total variation in 'y' that is explained by the relationship between y and x. It will be zero if there is no relationship; it will be between 0 and 1 if only part of the variation in 'y' is explained by the relationship; it will be 1 if all the variation in 'y' is explained (Bancroft & O'Sullivan, 1993).

These statistical tools help us determine the strength of the relationships found in the regression analysis, and thus help us reach a more accurate conclusion.

4. NON-PARAMETRIC TESTS (RUNS TESTS)

The runs test is used because both regression and correlation results can be influenced by extreme observations (Hui, 2005). The runs test only takes into consideration the signs of daily returns, and not their magnitude. This is done by replacing positive price changes with + and negative price changes with - (Granger & Morgenstern, 1970, p. 80).

A run is a sequence of one or the other symbol; thus the series '+++ ----- ++++' consists of three runs. According to the original technique developed by Cowles (1960) the number of sequences and reversals in the series of + and - signs (where sequence is either ++ or -- and reversal is +- or -+) should be roughly equal if the changes are independent of each other. This method however is affected by trends in the market which bias the data (see Granger & Morgenstern, 1970, p. 81).

END NOTE

The Efficient Market Hypothesis is an economic / investment theory according to which stock market efficiency causes existing share prices to always reflect all relevant information, making it impossible for traders to make abnormal profits by either purchasing undervalued stocks or selling stocks for inflated prices.

Thus, it should be impossible to outperform the market through fundamental or technical analysis, i.e. the only way a trader can possibly obtain higher returns is by purchasing riskier investments.

While the theory is sound, there is a large body of research that point to market inefficiencies, indicating that especially in less developed markets there are opportunities for abnormal returns.

Moreover, while the theory is economic, the concept depends on human rational behaviour and touches upon such areas as governance, the legal and regulatory framework, sociology, human perception etc.

Any business student will certainly come across the Efficient Market Hypothesis but the study on the subject will probably be confined to discussion of the theory. Research into its practical application is usually a topic for a thesis, most probably Weak Form Efficiency, especially at undergraduate level, while higher levels of efficiency are usually researched at postgraduate level due to the complexity and time required for effective research.

As we have seen, Weak Form Efficiency is challenged by anomalies such as the Day-of-the-Week. These anomalies imply that stock returns are not homogeneously distributed over the days of the week, or over specific times in the day. Several suggestions have been put forward to explain these anomalies, some of which suggest that they are not anomalies at all but logical consequences of other factors. However no conclusive evidence exists to date.

REFERENCES & BIBLIOGRAPHY

1. Bodie, Z., A. Kane & A. Marcus (1996), <u>Investments</u>, 3rd edition. Boston, MA: McGraw-Hill.

2. Elsharkawy, A. & N. Garrod (1996), 'The Impact of Investor Sophistication on Price Responces to Earnings News', <u>Journal of Business Finance & Accounting</u>, Vol. 23, No. 2, pp. 221-241.

3. Fama, E.F. (1965), 'Random Walks in Stock Market Prices', <u>Financial Analysis Journal</u>, January-Febueary 1995, pp. 75-80.

4. Fama, E.F. (1991), 'Efficient Capital Markets: II', <u>The Journal of Finance</u>, Vol. 46, No. 5, pp. 1575-1617.

5. Hand, J.R.M. (1990), 'A Test of the Extended Functional Fixation Hypothesis', <u>The Accounting Review</u>, Vol. 65, pp. 764-780.

6. Harris, L. (1986), 'A Transactions Data Study of weekly and Intradaily Patterns in Stock Returns', <u>Journal of Financial Economics</u> (May 1986), pp. 99-117.

7. Hourvouliades, N. L. (2009), New Evidence for the Day-of-The-Week Effect in the Financial Crisis, <u>International Conference on Applied Economics</u> (2009), pp. 225-244.

8. Lakonishok, J. & E. Maberly (1990), 'The Weekend Effect: Trading Patterns of Individual and Institutional Investors', <u>Journal of Finance</u> (Mar. 1990), pp. 231-243.

9. Lakonishok, J. & M. Smidt (1989), 'Are Seasonal Anomalies Real? A Ninety Year Perspective', <u>Review of Financial Studies</u>, Vol. 2, pp. 403-425.

10. Lucey, B. M. (1994), 'Some Empirics of the ISEQ Index', <u>Economic and Social Review</u>. Vol. 25, No. 2, pp. 157-77.

11.Lee, I., R.R. Pettit & M.V. Swankoski (1990), 'Daily Return Relationships Among Asian Stock Markets', Journal of Business Finance & Accounting, Vol. 17, No. 2, pp. 265-284.

12.Patell, J.M. & M.A. Wolfson (1982), 'Good News, Bad News and the Intraday timing of Corporate Disclosures', The Accounting Review (July 1982), pp. 509-527.

13.Penman, S.H. (1987), 'The Distribution of Earnings News Over Time and Seasonalities in Aggregate Stock Returns', Journal of Financial Economics (June 1987), pp. 199-228.

14.Rystrom, D.S. & E.D. Benson (1988), 'Investor Psychology and the Day-of-the-Week Effect', Financial Analysis Journal (Sep/Oct. 1988), pp. 75-78

15.Rogalski, R. (1984), 'New Findings Regarding Day-of-the-Week Returns Over Trading and Non-trading Periods: A Note', Journal of Finance (Dec. 1984), pp. 1603-1614.

16.Smirlock, M. & L. Stark (1986), 'Day of the Week and Intraday Effects in Stock Returns', Journal of Financial Economics (Sep. 1986), pp. 197-210.

17.Santamases, M. (1986), 'An Investigation of the Spanish Stock Market Seasonalities', Journal of Business Finance & Accounting, Vol. 13, No. 2, pp. 267-276.

18.Ziemba, W.T. & S.L. Schwartz (1991), Invest Japan: The Structure, Performance and Opportunities of Japans Stock, Bond and Funds Markets, Chicago: Probus Publishing.

OTHER BOOKS BY THE AUTHOR

EFFICIENT MARKET HYPOTHESIS: Introduction to the Efficient Market Hypothesis for Business Students

VISION AND MISSION: Introduction to Vision and Mission for Business Students

PERCEPTION: Introduction to Perception for Business Students

PROJECT MANAGEMENT: Introduction to Project Management for Business Students

GROUPS IN ORGANISATIONS: Introduction to Work Groups for Business Students

MARKET EFFICIENCY: DAY OF THE WEEK EFFECT. Introduction to Weak Form Efficiency for Business Students

Visit my Amazon Author page **for further details on all my Books.**

http://www.amazon.com/Mario-Chinas/e/B00PCN1WFC/

MARKET EFFICIENCY: DAY OF THE WEEK EFFECT

Introduction to Weak Form Efficiency for Business Students

ISBN: 978-9925-7383-2-8

FIRST EDITION